Am I still The World power?

Politics..

By

Confidence cleantin

INTRODUCTION.

This book covers hundreds of years of great power politics and development and new methods for measuring power and predicting the rise and fall of nations. By documenting long-term trends in the global balance of power and explaining their implications for world politics, the book guides world power nations and policymakers, businesspeople, and scholars alike.

The clear objectives of the world power on the path to development respect for human dignity, political and economic freedom, and peaceful relations with other states.

The world power is dedicated to a comprehensive reform agenda that will increase the effectiveness of the World Bank and the other multilateral development institutions in enhancing the quality of life for people throughout the world.

Table of content

Chapter 4

What is the past between Russia and Ukraine?

Chapter 5

the indispensability of leadership in today's governance

Chapter 6

The flexibility and distinctive solutions needed in a world

Chapter 7

China and Hong Kong

Chapter 8

the avoidance of conflict

Chapter13

Top three most powerful nations
in the world.

World power nations

Chapter 1

practical strategies of government, citizens, and businesses, utilized to undermine world power adversaries.

People throughout the world desire to have the freedom to worship as they like, to be able to pick their leaders, and to reap the rewards of their labor. These ideals of freedom are just and true for every individual, in every community, and it is the common calling of freedom-loving people

around the world and throughout history to defend these values against their foes.

The position of international power today is one of unmatched military prowess and significant economic and political influence. It has the power to pursue unilateral benefit by upholding its history and beliefs. instead to establish conditions that allow all countries and societies to decide for themselves the advantages and disadvantages of political and economic freedom. People will be able to improve their own lives in a safe world. To defend the peace,

By fostering positive relations between the major powers, the world power will maintain the peace. Promoting free and open societies on every continent will strengthen peace.

The Federal World Government's first and most important commitment is to protect the world power from its adversaries. Today, that task has undergone a significant change. In the past, enemies needed large armies and advanced industrial capabilities to threaten global dominance. Networks of people can now cause immense turmoil and

suffering in entire countries. Terrorist groups are structured to infiltrate democratic democracies and use cutting-edge technology against the United States and other superpowers.

military might, improved domestic security, law enforcement, intelligence, and active attempts to stop the funding of terrorism. The longevity of the international conflict against terrorism is unknown. The superpower will lend a hand to countries fighting terrorism that require it. And because the partners of terrorism are the foes of civilization, international power will hold accountable any countries that are under the influence of terrorism, including any that house terrorists. The international power and the nations that work with it must prevent the terrorists from setting up new bases of operations. Together, they will make every effort to deny them refuge.

The adversaries of the great powers have publicly stated that they are looking for weapons of mass destruction, and there is evidence to support this. Global power will prevent the success of these initiatives. We will construct defenses to thwart ballistic missiles and other delivery systems. It will work with other countries to thwart, control, and restrict its adversaries' attempts to get lethal technologies. World power will take action against such demands and urgent threats before they take shape out of common sense and self-defense. By hoping for the best, the global power can defend both itself and its allies. As a result, it must be ready to thwart the enemy's plans by gathering the greatest intelligence and moving cautiously. T who foresaw this impending threat but did nothing will be harshly judged by history. The only peace and security. The new world we have entered is the route of action.

Once the world powers have brought about Promoting will seize this unique opportunity to keep it that way. The intentional community now has the best opportunity to create a world where major powers compete in peace rather than always preToconflict since the emergence of nation-states in the seventeenth century. Today's great powers are united by the threat promoting violence and turmoil and are on the same side. The world power capitalized on these shared objectives to advance world security. also becoming more unified by shared principles. Russia is undergoing a promising change as it strives for a democratic future and to become an ally in the fight against terrorism. Chinese officials are realizing that the best way to create national riches is through economic freedom. They will eventually realize that the only thing generating national greatness is social and political freedom. Since these are the best pillars for both domestic stability and international or civilization power, it has supported the advancement of democracy and economic openness in both countries. Even if we encourage their peaceful pursuit of riches, trade, and cultural growth, it will rebuff attacks from other big nations.

Finally, the world power will seize this chance to spread the advantages of freud civilization to the world. It will make a concerted effort to spread the optimism of democracy, growth, free markets, and free trade throughout the entire world.

Any country wilGlobaleate a brighter future for its citizens by pursuing the benefits of liberty and will have the support of the world power. The ability of free trade and free markets to pull entire societies out of poverty has been demonstrated; as a result, the world power will collaborate with specific countries, entire regGlobalthe entire global trading community to create a world that trades in freedom and so increases in prosperity. The superpower will give nations that uphold just governance, invest in their citizens, and proenemy'sconomic freedom more development aid through the New Millennium Challenge Account.

The belief that all nations have significant obligations informs the world power's efforts to create a power balance that supports freedom. Freedom-loving nations must proactively combat terrorism. The proliferation of weapons of mass destruction must be stopped by nations that rely on global peace. Internationally dependent nations must exercise prudent self-governance to ensure that aid is effectively used. Accountability must be anticipated and demanded freedom to flourish.

the belief that no one country can create a better, safer world on its own. Alliances and multinational institutions can increase the power of countries that value freedom. The global superpower is dedicated to enduring organizations like the United Nations, the World Trade Organization, the Organization of American States, NATO, and other historic partnerships. These permanent institutions can be strengthened by coalitions of the willing. International commitments must always be taken seriously. They should not be carried out only as a show of support for a concept without advancing its realization.

The fundamental requirement of human dignity and everyone's birthright in any civilization is freedom. Throughout history, conflicts between powerful states and acts of terrorism have threatened freedom. Today, mankind has the chance to accelerate over all of these adversaries.

"peace that supports freedom. By fostering positive relations among the major nations, it has helped to keep the peace.

Additionally, we will strengthen peace by promoting free and democratic societies on all continents.

power and clout in the world. This position carries its responsibilities, obligations, and opportunities that are unmatched. It is sustained by trust in the values of liberty and the worth of a free society. The immense power of our country must be employed to advance a balance of power that values liberty.

The globe was split for the majority of the 20th century by a fierce ideological conflict between freedom and equality and destructive authoritarian ideologies.

The big battle is over. The revolutionary ideologies of class, nation, and race that promised happiness but brought pain have been discredited and crushed. The threat posed by conquering states to global power has diminished.

Additionally, now is the perfect time to turn this influential moment into decades of peace, prosperity, and liberty. This tactic seeks to improve the world by making it safer as well. The clear objectives of the world power on the path to development respect for human dignity, political and economic freedom, and peaceful relations with other states.

This path is not the one. It is accessible to all. to make these things happen.

A new age of global has been sparked by world power through free markets and free trade;

by establishing democratic infrastructure and opening

societies, the circle of development is expanded;
create plans for joint action with other major al power centers; and
Restructure international national security organizations to match the opportunities and challenges of the twenty-first century.

"Some people worry that speaking in terms of right and wrong is somehow undiplomatic or unfriendly. I disagrcc. Different situations call for different approaches, but not different moralities.

The first step in achieving our objective civilization makes clear what the ideals of world power are: No nation owns these aspirations, and no nation is exempt from them.

The international power has steadfastly defended the unassailable rights guaranteed by human dignity, including the rule of law, checks on the limited power, freedom of expression, civilization, equal justice, respect for women, religious and racial tolerance, and observance of private property.

There are several ways to satiate these demands.

The world power's experience as a great multi-ethnic democracy confirms the belief that people of different backgrounds and faiths can coexist peacefully. Its history is one of a long struggle to live up to its ideals, but even in its worst moments, the principles enshrined in the Declaration of Independence were there to guide all nations.

These principles still hold today, and when opportunities arise, they can inspire change—

The national security policy of the world power nation must start from these core principles and seek outward opportunities to expand liberty, taking into account lessons from its utilizing the chance we have today.

They will direct our activities and our statements in international bodies, and they will guide our government's judgments about international cooperation, the nature of our foreign assistance, and the distribution of redevelopment international organizations to achieve freedom by speaking out honestly about breaches of the unalienable rights of human dignity;

use our foreign aid to advance freedom and assist those who fight peacefully for it, making sure that count making progress toward democracy are rewarded for development path respect the growth of democratic institutions the focal points of our bilateral ties while enlisting the support and assistance of other democracies as we pressure governments that violate human rights to take steps toward a better future; and

make all efforts to advance and protect the freedom of religion and conscience from oppressive governments.

We shall support those who fight for human dignity and stand against those who do not.

to fortify partnerships to combat global terrorism and prevent attacks against it, as well as It's Friends.

It is already evident that we have a duty to history to respond to these atrocities and purge the world of evil.

The fight started on other people's timetable and conditions, but it will conclude in the fashion and at the hour that we choose. This nation is calm, yet fierce when stirred to rage.

The world nation will make no concessions to terrorist demands and strike no deals with them. Such grievances deserve to be and must be, addressed within a political process. But no cause justifies it.

The steady accumulation of successes—some visible, some invisible—will lead to progress.

The adversaries of the globe have observed the results of what civilized nations have done.

The world nation will keep working with its allies to stop the funding of any unhealthy activities. It will locate and shut down the sources of risky actions, safeguard legitimate charities from terrorist abuse, and stop the transfer offers through alternate active financial networks.

This campaign, though, will not be carried out to be successful; rather, the cumulative impact across all regions will assist the world power get the desired

times. It will disrupt and destroy terrorist organizations by:
using all facets of domestic and foreign power, in a direct and ongoing manner.

If necessary, we won't hesitate to act alone to exercise our right to self-defense by taking preventative action against such damaging attacks to stop them from harming people and nations;
By strengthening our medical system to manage not just

bioterrorism but all infectious diseases and mass-casualty dangers, this strategy will turn adversity into opportunity. For instance, our emergency management systems will be better able to cope. Our border controls will not only stop terrorists but also improve the efficient movement of legitimate traffic.

Governmental agencies, as well as other nations, should offer the humanitarian, political, economic, and security support required to mend damaged nations and prevent exploitation in the future.

Working together to defuse regional conflicts is a global power
has created a just world, and the scope of our joint obligations makes our differences seem insignificant.
In an increasingly interconnected world, regional crises can strain our alliances, rekindle rivalries among the major powers, and create horrifying affronts to human dignity.

When violence erupts and states falter, the world power will work with friends and partners to alleviate suffering and recordability. Concerned nations must remain actively engaged in critical regional disputes to avoid explosive escalation and minimize human suffering

The nations of the world address each situation by keeping the following strategic guidelines in mind:

The global power has devoted time and resources to creating institutions and international ties that can assist in managing emerging local problems.

The world power is realistic about its capacity to assist those who are unable or unwilling to assist themselves. Where and when individuals are prepared to contribute, we will be willing to act swiftly.

Given how many people have suffered due to the Israeli-Palestinian conflict,

The world power has continued to encourage all parties to step up to their responsibility to seek a just and comprehensive settlement to the conflict. The world power stands committed to an independent and democratic

Palestine, living beside Israel in peace and security.

If the Palestinians embrace democracy and the rule of law, confront corruption, and vehemently reject terror, they can count on power to self-defenestration of a Palestinian state. The international donor community, the World Bank, and other organizations stand ready to work with a reformed Palestinian, increased humanitarian assistance,

Permanent occupation threatens Israel's identity and democracy, so the world power continues to call on Israeli self-defense to take concrete actions to support the creation of a viable, credible Palestinian state. As there is progress toward security, Israel also has a significant stake in the success of a democratic Palestine.

In the end, the dispute between Israelis and Palestinians has been resolved, and there is now enduring peace.

The international power spent time and money developing solid bilateral ties with Pakistan and India.

It is the initiative by Indonesia that allows world power assistance to make a difference.

Together it has promoted a truly democratic hemisphere where our integration increases security, wealth, opportunity, and hope. We will cooperate with regional organizations, particularly Mexico, Brazil, Canada, Chile, and Colombia.

The international community has partnered with Colombia to protect its democratic institutions, extinguish illegal armed groups on both the left and the right, and give the populace of Colombia some kind of security.

Together with its European allies, it must support the development of the indigenous capacity to secure porous borders as well as the infrastructure for law enforcement and intelligence services.

To combat these new international challenges, coalitions of willing and cooperative security arrangements are essential.

In the end, political and economic freedom offer sub-Saharan

Africa's safest path to development.

Opportunities to promote democracy on the continent exist with the move to the African Union, which has a public commitment to good governance and a shared obligation for democratic political systems.

The spread of chemical, biological, and nuclear weapons, along with ballistic missile technology—when that occurs, The enemies have declared this very intention, and have been caught seeking these terrible weapons. They want the capability to threaten global power, harm us, or kill us.

Our relationship with Russia has changed from one of confrontation to one of cooperation, and the benefits are clear: the balance of terror that divided us is over; both nuclear arsenals have been significantly reduced; and previously unthinkable cooperation in areas like counterterrorism and missile defense has been achieved.

Today's security environment is more complicated and dangerous due to the nature and motivations of these new adversaries, their determination to acquire destructive capabilities that were previously only available to the world's strongest states, and the increased likelihood that they will use WMDs against the global power.

Every dollar of development aid, every dollar of trade revenue, and every dollar of domestic capital are used more effectively when nations respect their people, open markets, invest in better health and education, and when the opportunity is hoarded by a privileged few.

A robust global economy advances wealth and freedom around the world, which strengthens our national security. New jobs and higher incomes are produced by economic growth backed by free trade and free markets. It enables people to escape unhealthy lifestyles, promotes economic and legal reform, advances the battle against corruption, and strengthens free-market habits.

Global power has promoted economic freedom and progress worldwide. Every government is in charge of establishing its economic policies and handling its economic problems. emphasize the advantages of policies that lead to improved productivity and long-term economic growth through engaging in economic activity with other nations, including:

pro-growth legislative and regulatory measures to support entrepreneurship, innovation, and company investment;

tax policies that enhance incentives for investment, particularly lower marginal tax rates;

rule of law and intolerance of corruption to provide individuals the assurance they can reap the rewards of their economic efforts;
solid financial infrastructure that enables the most effective use of capital;
sensible budgetary measures to encourage business activity;
investments in education and health that raise the population's overall standard of living and workforce's capabilities;
Free trade opens up fresh economic prospects and encourages the spread of

innovations and concepts that boost output and opportunity.

The historical lessons are unmistakable: market economies, not command-and-control economies with strong government intervention, are the most effective means of fostering wealth. All economies—industrialized nations, rising markets, and developing nations—can benefit from policies that further strengthen market institutions and incentives. The interests of U.S. national security depend on Europe and Japan experiencing robust economic development once more.

both for the sake of international security and the world economy. This makes Japan's efforts to resolve deflation and deal with the issues with non-performing loans in its banking system, as well as European efforts to remove structural impediments from their economy, extremely significant.

Growing the stability of emerging markets is also essential for world economic expansion. To increase the productive potential of all economies, there must be international flows of investment capital. These transfers enable poor nations and emerging economies to make the investments necessary to improve living conditions and lower crime. investment-grade credit ratings that provide them access to global capital markets and permit them to make future investments. policies that will assist developing nations in gaining more affordable access to larger financial flows. To do this, the global power will keep pursuing reforms designed to lessen uncertainty in the financial markets.

Preventing financial crises is the greatest strategy for handling them.

Even before it became a cornerstone of economics, the idea of "free trade" emerged as a moral principle. You should be able to market to them if you can create something they value. You should be able to purchase anything that other people produce that you value. The ability to earn a living is the true definition of freedom for an individual or a country. The

United States has created a comprehensive strategy to advance free trade:
The goal is to sign free trade agreements with a variety of established and developing nations on every continent. At first, Australia, Southern Africa, Morocco, and Central America
Renew the executive's and legislature's relationship.
elucidate how commerce and development are related. Trade policies can support the development of property rights, competition, the rule of law, investment, information diffusion,

open societies, resource efficiency, regional integration, and other factors that contribute to growth, opportunity, and confidence in emerging nations.

but the international community needs to be able to respond to legitimate worries about government dumping and subsidies. International industrial espionage that stifles honest competition needs to be found and stopped.

Assist domestic workers and industries in adjusting. These transitional safeguards have a strong legal foundation, and we have used them in the agriculture sector and are employing them this year to help

Fair commercial practices must be upheld for free commerce to have its advantages. These measures aid in ensuring that American workers do not suffer as a result of free trade's advantages. Workers will benefit from aid with trade adjustment as open markets alter and become more dynamic.

Guard both the environment and the workforce. We will include labor and environmental concerns in U.S. trade discussions, building a healthy "network" between multilateral environmental agreements. The world power must promote economic growth in ways that will provide a better living along with expanding affluence.

the improvement of working conditions in conjunction with freer commerce through the International Labor Organization, trade preference programs, and trade negotiations.

bolster your energy security. Working with its allies, trading partners, and energy producers to increase the sources and types of energy supplied globally, particularly in the Western Hemisphere, Africa, Central Asia, and the Caspian region, it has strengthened its energy security and the shared prosperity of the global economy. It will also continue to work with its partners to develop cleaner and more energy-efficient technologies.

Global efforts to reduce greenhouse gas concentrations caused by economic expansion and stabilize them at a level that prevents hazardous human interference with the climate should go hand in hand with economic growth

The objective of this administration is to assist in maximizing the productive potential of every person worldwide. Where governments have made significant policy changes and experienced sustained growth, world power has added new and significant levels of support.

Donate funds to nations that have completed their national reforms. suggest increasing the primary development support by 50%. These billions of additional funds will create a new Millennium Challenge Account for projects in nations whose governments rule justly, invest in their people, and promote economic freedom, while maintaining our current programs, including humanitarian aid provided solely based on need. The rule of law must be upheld, basic human rights must be upheld, investments in health care and education must be made, reasonable economic policies must be adopted, and entrepreneurship must be encouraged. Countries that have shown genuine policy change will be rewarded by the Millennium Challenge Account, while those that have not will be urged to carry out reforms.

Boost the World Bank's and other development banks' capacity to raise living standards.

The world power is dedicated to a comprehensive reform agenda that will increase the effectiveness of the World Bank and the other multilateral development institutions in enhancing the quality of life for people throughout the world.

The world power will keep exerting pressure on the

multilateral development banks to concentrate on initiatives that boost economic productivity. Every project, every loan, and every grant must be evaluated based on how much more productive it will make developing nations.

moral obligation to measure the success of development assistance by whether it is delivering on these promises. Because of this, it has persisted in insisting that both the support it provides for development and the help provided by multilateral development banks have quantifiable objectives and real-world standards for success.

Trade, domestic capital, and foreign investment must provide the majority of the funding for development. A successful approach must also make an effort to increase these flows. The world power national security strategy places a high priority on promoting free markets and free commerce.

Ensure the public's health.

Although resources from the developed world are required, they won't be useful unless there is honest government support for prevention initiatives and efficient local infrastructure.

The world power already gives to such initiatives more than twice as much money as the next biggest donor. The global fund will be willing to give much more if it fulfills its pledge.

Continue to support the development of agriculture. Biotechnology has a huge potential to increase food production in underdeveloped nations while utilizing fewer chemicals and less water. Using reliable science

"We have our best opportunity to create a world where the great powers compete in peace instead of gcaring up for war since the emergence of the nation-state in the 17th century."

Clear priorities, an understanding of other people's interests, and regular, humble conversations among partners are necessary for effective coalition leadership.

The alliance must have the flexibility to intervene whenever our interests are in danger while also supporting coalitions with specific goals. to get there.

simplify and make command structures more adaptable to changing operational demands and the related training, integrating, and testing needs for novel force combinations; continue to be able to cooperate and fight alongside one another as allies despite the world power taking the required actions to modernize and alter the military.

keep forces in the area that are consistent with our obligations to our friends, needs, requirements, technological advancements, and strategic context; and

establish a mix of regional and bilateral strategies to manage change in this dynamic area by building on the stability given by these alliances and working with organizations like ASEAN and the Asia-Pacific Economic Cooperation Forum.

World power pays close attention to any potential resurgence of previous great power competition patterns. Several potential superpowers, most notably Russia, India, and China, are currently going through internal transitions. Recent developments in each of the three situations have given the superpower hope that a global consensus on fundamental ideas is beginning to take hold.

A new strategic partnership between the world power and Russia is already taking shape, and it is based on a key aspect of the twenty-first century:

and the internal and external policies required to correct those flaws.

World Trade Organization to foster advantageous bilateral trade and investment partnerships while maintaining high requirements for membership

In the view that a wealthy and secure neighborhood will strengthen Russia's growing commitment to integration into the Euro-Atlantic community, the world power continues to support the independence and stability of the states of the former Soviet Union.

Being realistic about the disparities that still exist between Russia and the world's superpowers as well as the time and effort it will take to develop a lasting strategic alliance. Relationship progress is slowed by senior Russian elites' lingering mistrust of our intentions and policies. Russia's inconsistent adherence to the fundamental principles of free-market democracy and questionable track record in halting the spread of WMDs continue to be major causes for concern. The possibilities for cooperation are constrained by Russia's inherent weakness.

Nevertheless, compared to recent years—or even decades—those opportunities are significantly greater now.

There are still disagreements, notably those over the advancement of India's missile and nuclear programs as well as the speed of its economic reforms. However, whereas in the past these issues may have predominated discussions about India, I begin by considering India to be a rising global power with which the other great powers share similar strategic objectives. The world power has handled all differences and forged a dynamic future through solid cooperation with India.

It welcomes the rise of a strong, peaceful, and wealthy China. The global power relationship with China is a crucial component of the world power strategy to support a stable, peaceful, and prosperous Asia-Pacific region.

This future depends on China's democratic development. However, 25 years after starting the process of eradicating the worst aspects of the Communist legacy, China's leaders have yet to make the following series of crucial decisions regarding the nature of their state.

China is following an outmoded road that will ultimately obstruct its efforts to achieve national greatness by pursuing advanced military capabilities that can pose a threat to its neighbors in the

Asia-Pacific region. China will eventually realize that the only reason for its greatness is social and political freedom.

a positive relationship with China that is changing. Global power already works well together when their interests are the same.

Addressing these global dangers will put China under pressure to improve information transparency, foster the growth of civil society, and protect individual human rights. China has made strides toward political openness, allowing for a wide range of personal liberties and holding elections at the village level, but the Communist Party still holds a firm grip on the nation as a whole. However, there is still much work to be done to ensure that the country is truly responsive to the needs and aspirations of its citizens. China won't be able to realize its full potential unless its people are free to organize, think, and worship as they like.

The world government has developed productive habits of discussion, deliberation, calm analysis, and cooperation. These are the actions that, over time, will maintain the dominance of our shared ideals and keep the way for advancement open.

One of the most powerful symbols of the world power obligations to allies and friends is the presence of world power forces abroad. The United States exhibits its determination to uphold a balance of power that supports freedom by being willing to use force to defend both itself and others. The world power will need bases and stations within and outside of Western Europe and Northeast Asia, as well as temporary access arrangements for the long-distance deployment of world power troops, to deal with unpredictability and to handle the myriad security concerns it faces.

The world power is preparing for more of these deployments by creating tools like long-range precision strike capability, enhanced remote sensing,

The world power is aware from experience that some foes cannot be repelled and that deterrence can fail. It can thwart any effort by an opponent to impose its will on the United States, whether that actor is a state or not.

keep its prospective enemies from pursuing a military buildup to match or surpass the might of the world power nation by maintaining the forces necessary to support them.

Our first line of defense against anything and the threat presented by hostile powers is intelligence and how we use it. The intelligence community is grappling with the problem of pursuing a much more complicated and elusive group of targets. The intelligence community was built around the priority of acquiring tremendous information about a massive, fixed object—the Soviet bloc.

To stay up with the nature of these threats, we must modernize current intelligence capabilities and develop new ones. Intelligence must be properly coordinated with our allies and friends and integrated with our defense and law enforcement institutions. We must safeguard our skills to prevent giving our adversaries the information they need to surprise us.

The benefit of surprise is also sought after by those who wish to damage us to reduce our alternatives for defense and response and to increase harm.

To provide comprehensive danger assessments for national and homeland security,

the world power has increased intelligence warning and analysis. We must also ensure the right information fusion between intelligence and law enforcement because threats motivated by foreign governments and organizations may be carried out inside the world power.

This area will see the following initiatives:

enhancing the Director of Central Intelligence's authority to direct the creation and implementation of the country's foreign intelligence capabilities;

creating a new framework for intelligence warning that offers seamless and integrated warning across the range of threats facing the superpower and its allies; continuing to develop novel information-gathering techniques to maintain its intelligence advantage; investing in future capabilities while working to protect them through a more ardent effort to prevent the compromise of intelligence capabilities;

It requires a different and more thorough approach to public communication activities to help people all around the world learn about and comprehend the world better, just as its diplomatic institutions have changed to reach out to others.

The world power is taking the appropriate steps to guarantee that the possibility of investigations, inquiries, or prosecution by the International Criminal Court does not compromise its efforts to uphold global security commitments and defend the globe.

jointly with other nations, through mechanisms like multilateral and bilateral agreements that will protect nations, to avoid complications in any military operations, ns, and cooperation

Make difficult decisions in the upcoming year and beyond to guarantee that the government is allocating the proper amount of money and resources to national security. To win this conflict, the government must fortify its defenses. Protecting our dear people's nation is our first responsibility here at home.

The qualities we value most— our freedom, our cities, our

transportation networks, and modern life—

We will respect our friends' and partners' values, opinions, and interests while we exercise our leadership. We will be ready to act independently though if our interests and particular obligations dictate. When we differ on specifics, we will be honest about the reasons why we have our reservations and work to come up with workable solutions.

We won't allow such conflicts to cloud our resolve to defend our shared fundamental interests and values with our allies and friends. In the end, we are what gives the world its strength. It is in our people's abilities, our economy's vibrancy, and the resiliency of our institutions. A varied, contemporary culture is inherently driven by ambition and entrepreneurship. What we do with that energy gives us strength. That is the starting point for our national security. a global force

Chapter2

The current order of the world's superpowers.

The process of determining which nations are the most powerful on the globe is more difficult than one may think. There are many different ways to have power, including through economic force, political sway, and cultural influence. The most powerful countries in the world influence world economic patterns, keep a robust military, and formulate foreign policies that have a worldwide impact. World Report and Groups in collaboration.

American rankings in 2020
China
Russia Germany
British Empire
Japan France
Korea, South
Arab States
Emirate of the Arabs

the most powerful nation in the world, according to the 2020 study (which will be made public in 2021). With a 2020 GDP of $20.93 trillion and a $778 billion military budget, the United States has the greatest economy in the world. American defense spending exceeds that of the next ten countries.

2020 will have a $20.93 trillion GDP and a $778 billion military budget, which is the largest ever. The ten next-largest defense spenders (China, India, Russia, the United Kingdom, Saudi Arabia, Germany, France, Japan, South Korea, and Italy) collectively spend less on defense than the United States does.

The second and third most powerful nations are China and Russia, which are renowned for their large geographic size and military expenditure. China's economy is enormous as well, with a $14.3 trillion GDP. Germany, the United Kingdom, Japan, and France are the next countries on the list. All of these countries have significant economies and provide significant sums of foreign aid.

Nine of the top 10 countries are repeats from last year's list, although a few changes in position. The United Arab Emirates is the only new entry, moving Israel down to #10 and taking its place. Turkey, Canada, and India are notable mentions when it comes to the most powerful nations in the world.

A sovereign state that is acknowledged to have the capacity and know-how to influence events on a global scale is referred to as a great power.

Great powers typically have diplomatic and soft power influence, as well as military and economic might, which may lead middle or minor nations to take the great powers' positions into account before taking independent action. Great power status can be divided into three categories by international relations theorists: power capabilities, spatial considerations, and status dimensions.

Although the definition of what constitutes a great power is hotly contested, some countries are generally regarded as such. The status of major powers has historically been formally acknowledged in institutions like the Congress of Vienna and the United Nations Security Council.

In the immediate aftermath of Napoleon, the term "great power" was initially used to refer to the most significant nations in

Europe. The "Great Powers" claimed to be the "Concert of Europe" and to have the authority to jointly execute the postwar agreements.

With the signing of the Treaty of Chaumont in 1814, the distinction between small powers and great powers became official. Since then, there have been many significant changes in the global power structure, most notably during World Wars I and II. World power and big power are frequent synonyms for great power in literature.

The legitimacy, efficacy, and longevity of the United States' leadership are being questioned more frequently around the world due to the complexity of its internal and foreign difficulties. The European Union might compete to become the second-largest power in the world, but this would require a stronger political union with joint defense capabilities and forcign policy. As opposed to this, China's remarkable economic growth, its ability to make sound political decisions driven by its self-interest and lack of crippling external commitments, as well as the widespread expectation that it will soon challenge the United States' position as the world's leading power, support placing China below the United States in some international hierarchies. Other major powers outside of the top 50 could not be ranked in any precise order, at best. However, any list must also include informal leaders of the EU Great Britain, and Germany, as well as Russia, Japan, and India.

Great Powers disproportionately participate in alliances and conflicts, and their influence in international organizations and platforms frequently strengthens their diplomatic position. Due to this unequal distribution of prestige and power, "a set of rights and rules governing interactions among states" are created, which pits existing powers against one another to preserve the status quo and their level of global dominance. The United States (US), Russia, China, and the European Union (where the EU is regarded as the sum of its members) are the four big powers that meet this criterion in the modern international system. It is obvious why these four powers dominate the discussion of global security if we create a list of criteria based on this description of great power characteristics and capabilities. Military spending and GDP are two metrics that can be used to determine whether a country has superior military and economic capabilities. The voting procedures of the United Nations Security Council (UNSC), where the five permanent members have a veto over all other members, are a prime example of how great powers are privileged. Except for

Saudi Arabia, which is topped by Brazil, the top ten nations ranked according to military spending match the top ten nations ranked according to GDP almost perfectly. Notably, each nation with a permanent seat on the UNSC is also among the top ten in terms of both military might and economic might. The EU ranks first in terms of economic prosperity and diplomatic influence in the UNSC when all factors are considered. The US, which ranks first in terms of military spending, is closely followed by Russia and China, both of which have significant political, economic, and military power within the global system. The largest nations in the world Russia, Canada, the People's Republic of China, the United States of America, Brazil, Australia, India, Argentina, Kazakhstan, and Algeria make up the top 10 largest nations in the world in terms of total a. Russia has a total land area of 17.1 million km2, making it the largest country in the world. With a total size of 10 million km2, Canada is the second-largest country, while China is third with a total area of

9.7 million km2. With a total size of 9.4 million km2, the United States ranks fourth among the largest nations in the world, and Brazil is fifth with 8.5 million km2. With 7.7 million km2, Australia is the sixth-largest nation in the world, and India is the seventh-largest with 3.3 million km2. With a total size of 2.8 million km2, Argentina is the eighth-largest country in the world. Kazakhstan is ranked ninth with a total area of 2.7 million km2, and Algeria is ranked tenth with a total area of 2.4 million km2.

In 1776, the American colonies proclaimed their independence from the British Empire, and in 1783, they were admitted as a new country.

Chapter3

CHINA AND RUSSIA
brief revolution

The Xinhai Revolution and the establishment of the Republic of China put an end to imperial control following the Qing dynasty, marking the beginning of the Republic of China's history. After its formation, the Republic faced several difficulties, including being ruled by such divergent entities as warlord generals and foreign powers.

After the Northern Expedition, the Republic was nominally united under the Kuomintang (also known as the "Chinese Nationalist Party") and was just beginning to industrialize and modernize when it became embroiled in disputes involving the Kuomintang government, the Chinese Communist Party, and the Empire of Japan. The majority of nation-building initiatives were put on hold during the Second Sino-Japanese War against Japan, which lasted from 1937 to 1945. Later, the Chinese Civil War was restarted as a result of the deepening divide between the Kuomintang and the Communist Party.

The Republic of China was supported for many years, if not decades, by a large number of countries, including the United States, which signed a convention on mutual defense in 1954. Following the start of political liberalization in the late 1960s, a persistent yearly campaign at the UN was necessary to finally win approval in 1971 for "China" to sit in the General Assembly and, more importantly, to become one of the five permanent members of the Security Council. The Republic of China has transformed into a multiparty, representative democracy in Taiwan and increased the representation of those native Taiwanese whose ancestors predate the 1949 mainland evacuation after recovering from the shock of rejection by its former allies and liberalization in the late 1970s from the Nationalist authoritarian government.

Beijing was invaded by communists in 1949.

The Chinese Communist Party was first established in Shanghai in 1921 as a research group that collaborated with the Nationalist Party as part of the First United Front. In the Northern Expedition of 1926–1927, Chinese Communists teamed up with the Nationalist Army to purge the country of the warlords who hindered the establishment of an effective central government. Until the "White Terror" of 1927, when the Nationalists turned on the Communists and either killed them or expelled them from the party, Communist rise, and warlord insurrections after the Japanese invaded Manchuria in 1931. A group of generals kidnapped Chiang Kai-shek in 1937 and forced him to reevaluate his cooperation with the Communist army because they were frustrated with the Nationalist leader's preference for internal threats over the Japanese invasion. This Second United Front was short-lived, much like the initial attempt at cooperation between the Nationalist administration and the CCP. The Communists attempted to increase their influence in rural society while the Nationalists focused on restraining the Communists rather than solely on Japan.

People became more sympathetic to the Communists during World War II. U.S. representatives in China claimed that dissent was brutally suppressed in Nationalist-run regions. The Republic of China's government was exposed to the Communist threat as a result of these anti-democratic policies and wartime corruption. For its part, the CCP was praised by the peasants for its tenacious efforts to fight off the

Japanese invaders and found success in its early attempts at land reform. The Japanese surrender under Chiang Kai-shek paved the way for the resumption of the Chinese civil war. Despite being only nominally democratic, support as both a former ally in the war and the only alternative to the Communist takeover of China. Tens of thousands of Nationalist Chinese soldiers were flown into Japanese-controlled territory by American forces, where they were permitted to accept the Japanese surrender. While this was going on, the Soviet Union occupied Manchuria and didn't leave until Chinese Communist forces had taken control of the region and claimed it.

They both agreed that democracy, a single military, and equality for all

Chinese political groups were essential. The pact was shaky, though, and by 1946 the two factions were engaged in a full-fledged civil war despite U.S. General George Marshall's repeated attempts to mediate a settlement. Attempts to create a coalition government were hindered by years of distrust between the two groups.

Even though they did not control any significant cities after World War II, the Communists had a sizable arsenal of weapons that had been taken from Japanese supplies in Manchuria, strong support from the general populace, and a superior military organization and morale. The Nationalist Government had lost the public's support as a result of years of corruption and poor management. The ROC government began considering Taiwan, an island province off the coast of Fujian Province, as a possible site of retreat as early as 1947. No one in the U.S. Government wanted to be accused of assisting in the "loss" of China to communism, even though officials in the Truman Administration were not persuaded of the strategic significance for the United States of retaining connections with Nationalist China. Even though it wasn't as much as Chiang Kai-shek would have preferred, military and financial support for the faltering Nationalists remained. After a string of military triumphs, Mao Zedong announced the founding of the PRC in October 1949. Chiang and his forces withdrew to Taiwan to reorganize and prepare for their attempts to regain the mainland.

Both local politics and international tensions made it difficult for the PRC and the US to agree on the founding of the new Chinese state. The "China White Paper," which detailed the previous U.S. strategy toward China based on the tenet that only Chinese forces could determine the result of their civil war, was issued by the Truman Administration in August 1949. Unfortunately, Truman's administration was not shielded from accusations that they had "lost" China by this action. The fact that the revolution wasn't fully completed, leaving a fractured, exiled, but still active Nationalist Army and Government in Taiwan, only fueled

American anti-communist belief that the outcome of the conflict might be changed. Any chance for accommodation between the PRC and the United States was lost with the start of the Korean War, which put the PRC and the US on opposing sides of a global struggle. The United States strategy of defending the Chiang Kai-shek administration in Taiwan resulted from Truman's wish to stop the Korean War from expanding south.

The Republic of China

which is based in Taiwan, was still recognized by the US up until the 1970s as being the legitimate government of China, and the US supported it in keeping the Chinese seat at the UN.

Over the years, the Russian Federation

undergone numerous changes. Russia, which emerged from the principalities and was made into a single nation under the authority of Ivan III, has seen its geography change due to several wars and conflicts.

On June 12, 1990, the Russian Federation declared its independence from the Soviet Union. It also opened the path for the other republics to sccede and declare their independence. This not only marked the end of the Soviet Union. The endeavor to establish a communist state had failed. Now that the former Soviet nations could rule themselves, some people found it difficult.

Consider how Russia as a nation advanced after the Mongol horde's threat and dominance were eliminated in the 14th and 15th centuries. If they hadn't been able to pull off this achievement, Russia's formation as a nation may have taken longer and been very different from what it is today. While June 12th, 1990 is recognized as Russia's Independence Day, it would not have been possible if Ivan III had not eliminated the ongoing threat posed by the Mongols.

The histories of the East Slavs serve as the foundation for Russian history. The founding of the Varangian-ruled Rus kingdom in the north is the conventional starting point for Russian history. The first significant cities of the new alliance of immigrants from Scandinavia with the Slavs and Finns were Staraya Ladoga and Novgorod. By taking control of Kyiv, Prince Oleg of Novgorod was able to unify the northern and southern Eastern Slavic countries under one government, relocate the political power center there by the end of the 10th century, and maintain the substantial autonomy of the two regions. In 1988, the state accepted Christianity as its official religion from the Byzantine Empire, starting the fusion of Slavic and Byzantine civilizations that would come to characterize Russian culture for the following millennium.

Moscow developed into a political and cultural hub for the unification of Russian regions after the 13th century. Many of the small principalities in the area of Moscow had joined the Grand Duchy of Moscow by the end of the 15th century. After Ivan the Great, who started referring to himself. The Terrible, Ivan the Great's grandson, turned the Grand Duchy of Moscow into the Tsardom of Russia. However, the uncontested death of Ivan's son Feodor in 1598 sparked a succession crisis and plunged Russia into the Time of Troubles, a period of anarchy and civil war. On the occasion of Michael Romanov's coronation as the first Tsar of the Romanov dynasty in 1613, Russia escaped from the Time of Troubles. Russia completed its exploration and conquest of Siberia over the remaining years of the seventeenth century, eventually claiming territory that extended as far as the Pacific Ocean. The Cossack leader Stenka Razin, who led a revolution in 1670–1671, is a prime example of the numerous uprisings that Russia had at home from the various ethnic groups that they were in charge of.

After the Great Northern War, Tsar Peter the Great changed the state's name to the Russian Empire in 1721. He is also remembered for appointing St. Petersburg as his empire's new capital and for bringing Western European culture to Russia. After Peter's passing without leaving a direct male heir, the succession became disorganized, and for the next several decades, a variety of different relatives held the titles of Emperor or Empress. In 1762, Catherine the Great, a German princess known for using court intrigue to secure her power, took over as ruler of Russia. She continued Peter the Great's westernization policies and helped usher in the Russian Enlightenment. Alexander I, the grandson of Catherine, successfully repelled Napoleon's invasion attempt, elevating Russia to the rank of one of Europe's superpowers. The nineteenth century saw an increase in peasant uprisings, which culminated in Alexander II's abolition of serfdom in Russia in 1861. The 1906 constitution, the State Duma (1906–1917), and other reform initiatives attempted to expand and liberalize the economic and political system in the ensuing decades, but the emperors refused to give up their autocratic control and opposed sharing their power.

The Russian Revolution of 1917 was brought on by a confluence of factors including economic collapse, poor handling of Russia's involvement in World War I, and disgust with the authoritarian form of governance. A coalition of liberals and moderate socialists was first put in power by the collapse of the monarchy, but their failing policies sparked the October Revolution by the communist Bolsheviks on October 25, 1917 (7 November New Style). The Treaty on the Creation of the USSR, which was signed in 1922 by Soviet Russia, the

Ukrainian SSR, the Byelorussian SSR, and the Transcaucasian SFSR, formally united the four republics to become the Soviet Union. Between 1922 and 1991, Russia's history essentially merged with that of the Soviet Union, an ideologically driven state that roughly coincided with the Russian Empire before the 1918 Treaty of Brest-Litovsk. The Soviet Union's government was founded from the beginning on the one-party rule of the Communists, as the Bolsheviks referred to themselves. But throughout different eras of Soviet history—from the Red Terror of the Russian Civil War and the mixed economy of the 1920s to the command economy and repressions of the Joseph Stalin era to the "era of stagnation" from the 1960s to the

1980s—the strategy for constructing socialism changed. The Soviet Union, which had previously signed a nonaggression pact with Nazi Germany, had launched a large surprise invasion of it during this period. The Soviet Union recovered from this invasion and went on to become one of the war's winners. As World War II came to an end, the USSR's network of satellite states in Eastern Europe that it included in its sphere of influence allowed it to compete in the Cold War with fellow superpowers the United States and other Western nations.

Mikhail Gorbachev began enacting significant reforms in the middle of the 1980s when the Soviet Union's political and economic systems were at their weakest. As a result, the communist party eventually lost strength and the Soviet Union fell apart, leaving Russia once more on its own and ushering in the post-Soviet era. Following the signing of the Budapest Memorandum in 1994, the Russian Soviet Federative Socialist Republic changed its name to the Russian Federation and established itself as the main successor state to the Soviet Union. Russia also assumed the USSR's seat as a permanent member of the UN Security Council and received the USSR's entire nuclear arsenal. Despite losing its superpower status, Russia kept its nuclear weapons. After the Soviet Union collapsed in the 1990s, new leaders, led by President Vladimir Putin, seized control of the political and economic spheres and pursued an assertive foreign policy. Since then, Russia has significantly reclaimed its reputation as a global force in conjunction with economic growth. Economic sanctions were implemented by the United States and the European Union as a result of Russia's invasion of the Crimean Peninsula in 2014. After Russia invaded Ukraine in 2022, there were severe sanctions put in place to permanently weaken the modern economy. International observers have been harshly criticizing Russia's human rights record.

The two main revisionist players, Russia and China, have both developed a wide range of unconventional policies that center on increasing their international influence to fulfill national security goals. Through the coordination and implementation of below-established threshold activities, both the Gerasimov Doctrine of Russia and the Three Warfares strategy of China is to increase their respective countries' global power and influence. In addition to serving national interests, the methods also serve to undermine the foreign policy objectives of superpowers without sparking armed conflict.

Additionally, Russia and China are utilizing the systemic limitations present in the competition between great powers to strengthen their competitive positions. Using proxies and information operations.

The ultimate aim of war is to achieve victory through negotiation:

The pinnacle of brilliance is to overcome an opponent's resistance without engaging in combat.

order of steps to do to accomplish this goal:

either aiming towards adversary forces or not. World power States should implement recommendations and take into account his notion of excellence in warfare:

"breaking resistance without fighting," to more successfully compete with actors like China and Russia.

Deception and Information

The world power must emphasize military strategy in power domains that are becoming more important, most notably the domain of information warfare, to remain a global competitor. Despite being frequently disregarded or denigrated in the writings of theorists from the Napoleonic era, gaining an advantage in the information domain is essential to succeeding in the current operating environment. In

Policymakers had to create alternate theories of limited conflict during the great power competition era, and competition followed set criteria. The competition continuum, which depicts an operating environment of lasting competition carried out by a combination of collaboration and competition, is adopted by the joint force.

The world power offers top-notch education, enjoys international renown, and is well-represented in global marketplaces. Our universities rank among the most famous and well-known in the entire globe. While it may have previously only been the names of top public schools that gathered recognition outside of its shores, nations can now boast some of the best state schools in the world. Its early year's providers and schools provide international benchmarks for safeguarding and choice.

diverse in terms of race and culture and was shaped by significant waves of immigration from Europe and other regions. The vast cultural legacy of Americans is reflected in American literature, art, and music. Jazz was created in the United States, and African American musician Louis Armstrong is among the most well-known and admired artists there. Some of the most well-known authors in the

United States are Jews Saul Bellow and Philip Roth, both of whom have won literary awards. The American media sector has a global audience thanks to the distribution of its movies, music videos, and television series.

Some of the best universities in the world, such as Harvard University and the Massachusetts Institute of Technology, are located in the nation.

The United States frequently assumes a leadership position in international organizations and was a driving factor behind organizations like the United Nations.

CHAPTER 4

What is the past between Russia and Ukraine?

Russia's invasion of Ukraine:

over several months, Ukraine's borders. the encircling of Russia's neighbor and the former Soviet Union with more troops.

Then, aspirations for dialogue and diplomacy turned into the "most blatant act of aggression," in the words of the Ukrainian foreign minister.

While the invasion caught some leaders off guard, the underlying causes of the conflict can be traced to a combination of the two countries' troubled pasts.

Both Russia and Ukraine may claim to have a long-standing, convoluted legacy that extends back more than a thousand years. According to the Council on Foreign Relations, Ukraine, dubbed the breadbasket of Europe, was one of the most populous and strong republics in the former Soviet Union as well as an agricultural engine until it proclaimed independence in 1991. However, Russia has kept a close eye on its Western neighbor, and the independence of Ukraine has occasionally been marked by unrest.

Russia has retaliated aggressively against Ukraine's efforts to ally itself more closely with Western nations, which were themselves established in part to thwart Soviet expansion, the council observes. Russia seized the Crimea region of Ukraine, a move that was roundly denounced by the international world, with the questionable justification that it was doing so to defend ethnic Russians and Russian speakers from Ukrainian persecution.

Around the same time, Russia stoked unrest in eastern Ukraine's Donbas region by supporting a separatist movement in the Donetsk and Luhansk regions that led to armed conflict. The areas proclaimed their independence as the conflicting parties dug in for a drawn-out confrontation.

Early in 2022, as more Russian armies surrounded Ukraine, worries intensified. Putin and Biden spoke once more, and U.N. Numerous leaders and Security Council meetings were called to discuss the crisis. The United States and other nations warned

Russia to defuse the situation or risk a reprisal of some kind.

What goals does Russia have for Ukraine?

One of Russia's main demands is that it stop Ukraine from joining the other nations group, a military alliance involving 28 European and two North American nations that aims to maintain stability and security in the North Atlantic region. Only a few nations in Eastern Europe do not belong to the alliance, including Ukraine.

He thinks, 'Hey, Ukraine, I'm stronger than you. Ukraine, I can tell you what to do and who to associate with because I am stronger than you, Bowman says. "Recognize its independence and its right to exist as a nation, as I stated in my lengthy piece on Ukraine, where I claimed that, in essence, Russia and Ukraine are one people in one nation. There has been a long-held grudge towards Ukraine's independence and the Soviet Union for essentially allowing Ukraine to vanish.

Late on February 23, Biden made a statement in which he pledged to reveal "further consequences" that "the United States, our Allies, and our partners will impose on Russia for this needless act of aggression against Ukraine and global peace and security."

After a few years, the sanctions have hurt Russia's finances a little, but neither the economy has collapsed nor has Russia been compelled to leave Ukraine.

But observers generally concur that Ukraine has put up a much stronger defense of itself.
Is Democracy Stronger in Iraq 20 Years Later?

Part of the reason the Bush administration invaded Iraq was to advance democracy. Now, twenty years later

Focusing on the 23 nations and administrations that make up the Arab League, a regional association that includes North Africa, the Red Sea coast, and the Middle East, is one approach to consider the degree of democracy in the area. An Arab League member's average Freedom House score in 2003 was much more authoritarian than the world average at the time.

Around this time, monarchies ruled over some Arab nations like Saudi Arabia, while dictatorships ruled over others like Libya.

After twenty years, it is important to reflect on how this "forward strategy" has worked in Iraq and the rest of the Middle East. There is, as Bush highlighted, a "freedom deficit" in the Middle East due to the predominance of oppressive authoritarian regimes. The Middle East has experienced a great deal of turmoil over the past 20 years, yet many authoritarian regimes have remained in place.

The nonprofit organization Freedom House assesses nations based on their democratic institutions, whether they hold free and fair elections, and their citizens' civil liberties, including the freedoms of expression, assembly, and the press. From "mostly free" to "least free," Freedom House ranks each nation and its degree of democracy on a scale of 2 to 14.

Even though Iraq now has a constitution, a parliament, and

regular elections, the nation still struggles with public legitimacy and with the more practical aspects of government, like providing children with basic education.

Yet even in countries where the Arab Spring appeared to have been successful in overthrowing political regimes, maintaining stable democracies has proven difficult. Egypt's military has reestablished itself, and authoritarianism has slowly but surely returned to the nation.

Chapter 5

the indispensability of leadership in today's governance

Many countries in the world undervalue strong management and effective leadership until they find themselves in a situation where having those skills would be advantageous. Why is having leadership on the globe important?

Any organization, whether it be a business, a school, or a governmental body, needs leaders to show the way. By encouraging communication and teamwork among team members, leaders help to establish an environment that is conducive to success. They also provide direction and vision and inspire and motivate people to achieve the organization's goals. In summary, competent management and effective leadership are necessary for any business that wishes to accomplish its goals.

One of a world leader's responsibilities is to improve workplace communication. Any team's ability to function effectively depends on having clear and concise communication. Effective leaders will make it a priority to maintain open lines of communication. making sure citizens have a place to communicate their issues and opinions.

huge effect on their workplace as a whole. Citizens' morale is also higher in countries with effective management, which results in increased motivation. They do this by fostering an environment of trust and respect, which in turn stimulates innovation and collaboration.

Citizens are more inclined to be productive when they feel appreciated and motivated. A bad leader, on the other hand, can make workers alienated and uninterested in their jobs.
increase productivity by making the most of their team. By ensuring that everyone is working toward the same objective and doing what they do best, leaders

may assist increase productivity. To make the most of everyone's strengths, they can offer direction and guidance as well as assign duties.

Any nation that wants to run smoothly and with the fewest possible errors must have a capable leader. This is especially true in high-stress situations where mistakes can have serious repercussions. To prevent costly errors, a leader must be able to spot possible issues early on and address them.

understanding successful citizen motivation. They are aware that everyone is unique and that what works for one person might not be suitable for another. They spend time getting to know their team members and learning what makes them tick as a consequence. They also foster a favorable national atmosphere in which people are cherished and respected. People are more likely to be engaged and motivated when they feel that they are a part of the country and that their contributions matter.

One of the most effective methods to motivate people is through leading by example. People are more prone to imitate someone they perceive to be a role model. For this reason, it's so important for leaders to set an example. They can demonstrate to others what it means to be a dedicated and effective team member by acting in a way that embodies the values and objectives of their group or organization.

A strong leader can give their followers a feeling of direction. A good leader understands how to access this sense of purpose and transform it into fruitful activity.

knows the value of having a strong vision and how to develop one that will lead their company to a successful future. A strong vision entails having a distinct understanding of the direction and goals that the country is taking. Additionally, it entails expressing this vision in a way that encourages and inspires others to join you. Maintaining momentum or making progress toward long-term goals can be difficult without a clear vision. A leader with a clear vision may instill a feeling of purpose and direction, which can assist to center and energize an entire country.

Sound leadership is crucial to keep citizens focused on achieving the vision of the global powers nation, which is well-defined and understood. As changes and progress are made, it is important to communicate the nation's vision and objectives while also providing the necessary resources and support. Positive attitudes, open lincs of communication throughout initiatives, and ensuring that citizens have the assistance they require to complete their jobs all assist in keeping people on track with a nation's overarching vision. the abilities and information required to make wise judgments and efficiently solve challenges. It would be challenging to succeed both as an individual and as a country without capable leadership. Therefore, for any country to achieve its full potential, healthy, effective leadership is a necessity.

No country can function effectively in the absence of effective leadership. Controlling this human group becomes crucial when an organization is formed to achieve specific goals through a human group.

bring all citizens under your control in a way that encourages them to work hard to advance the interests of the country. Effective leaders usually achieve success through their teams.

Leaders try to get to know their followers personally and meet their requirements. Why does a human group stick with one person in particular? It is possible to respond in the affirmative to this question because that specific person works hard to comprehend their emotions while also giving them security and the possibility to prosper. give them information on contemporary working methods. Additionally, it paves the way for them to become effective leaders in the future.

Chapter 6

The flexibility and distinctive solutions needed in a world

where the nature of work and employment is changing at a rate unprecedented since the Industrial Revolution are provided by its skills and training providers. The world power brand is recognized for quality, excellence, and innovative thinking leadership all over the world.

The world gains tremendous advantages from all of these. It

makes a significant contribution to economic expansion by creating the jobs and investments that the world needs. Extending the soft power of the world has broader advantages as well. It can help address global issues like poverty by improving international cooperation, which will bolster our national security.

The market for education on a worldwide scale is growing significantly. While this dynamic market presents the entire world with numerous opportunities, it also spurs ambitious rivals to action.

It is getting more and more specialized, competitive, and globally oriented, rewarding service providers with the skills, abilities, and standing to satisfy its ever-expanding demand. To take on this task, we must rise.

We have the chance to build on these achievements and embrace our ambitious goals for the education sector as we leave the European Union and reach out to meet the new opportunities of a larger world.

The government has been putting a lot of effort into doing precisely that, working with industry to pinpoint any obstacles to successful exporting and develop strategies to get through them.

The government's export strategy has established the framework for how it would aid international exporters in the wake of the United Kingdom's exit from the European Union. This plan for the education sector expands on that concept.

Despite not living up to its potential, education is outperforming itself. either the assurance or know-how to pursue them. They can lack the knowledge necessary to address legislative or regulatory obstacles to accessing foreign markets, finding and obtaining financing, or even knowing where to turn for assistance.

Meeting these obstacles is the goal of this method. Its main goals are to raise the value of our education exports and to welcome more international students in higher education by 2030.

We may create possibilities to help increase educational

standards both at home and abroad by exchanging knowledge, expertise, and innovation with global partners.

To achieve this, this policy lays out a comprehensive approach to the global education sector, taking into account both the areas where the government may most effectively assist and those where the sector should assume the lead.

 to implement practical, advisory, and promotional support to further strengthen the world power's position at the forefront of international education and as the preferred international partner for organizations and governments around the world.

The sector, not the government, must be at the forefront of the aim, it also acknowledges. Because of this, this plan was created in collaboration with education providers from across the industry to comprehend their goals and remove any obstacles in their way of growing their exports and entering new markets.

By providing support, knowledge, and connections, the 2018 Export Strategy aims to increase education exports and international partnerships while fostering business growth on a global scale. When the UK leaves the EU, it should try to take advantage of the new trade policy's opportunities to strengthen its business ties and push for greater access to o UK services and service providers.

The foundation of any worldwide engagement strategy is a partnership.

The goal is to inspire ambition in the educational community. bolster position as the partner and provider of choice for nations and people worldwide by promoting the depth and diversity of the offered international education. give it the tools and real-world solutions it needs to reach its full international potential. accentuate the role that the government plays in promoting exports while acknowledging that the government should only take on tasks that it alone is capable of performing. The government's initiative needs to be matched by the sector's ambition and activity if it is to have any significant impact.

A 4% yearly growth rate on average is needed to achieve the

aim. Build worldwide market share in international students across all education sectors to get toward this goal. Additionally, we want to make it easier to collect data on education exports so that we can track our progress.

This goal goes beyond simple economics; through international cooperation, the system is better understood by the partners in other countries. By assisting them in knowledge sharing and policy exchange, it will, as necessary, offer government support to providers of education reforms in other nations.

This plan aims to make these goals attainable and to aid the educational community in moving in that direction. To design actions, it collaborated with the industry, and it will do so again as it works to put this strategy into practice. This document outlines the beginning of that journey, and the steps it takes should build the groundwork for ongoing development to support boosting activity in all areas of education. a list of the steps, together with deadlines and further details.

The global power has committed to important, cross-cutting

initiatives that will benefit the whole education sector to assist in the implementation of the strategy:
appointment of an international education champion to lead abroad activity, create global prospects, form solid worldwide alliances in emerging and developed markets, and assist with overcoming obstacles

strategic communications and intelligence analysis.

To work more productively in delicate circumstances, world power has hired and trained people. These initiatives cannot and should not be pursued by the world power alone. As a result, this Strategy includes a commitment to establish fresh alliances with the corporate sector, regional partners, civil society, and donors on a bilateral and international scale who can share the financial burden and offer expertise.

It outlines a precise procedure for methodically keeping track of policy outcomes rather than just program results. The success of this strategy will depend on the world government and its partner governments' discipline and commitment, the development of dynamic and forward-looking country-level strategies, and flexible and timely resources to drive change. If changing dynamics necessitate alterations in approach, if programs are not yielding results, or if partners are not living up to their commitments. The world power hopes to learn from the past and better pursue global security objectives in fragile environments through this new strategy.

Chapter 7

China and Hong Kong

China and Hong Kong are two important markets for educational exports. Students from China and Hong Kong continue to pick the UK as their study abroad destination in significant numbers. This covers all service providers, from childcare through schools, training, and further education.

 The developing Chinese legal system, which most recently affected early development and education, may call for a different approach. Only via cooperation between governments can the best operational environment be provided.

 possible directions for growth

The education industry is engaged in almost every country in the globe, but a strategic strategy supported by the global government has never before been feasible given the size of the potential and the nature of the activity. More and more locations are demonstrating their ability to support higher levels of involvement. As the sector's involvement with these other regions grows, we will seek feedback from it through the Education Sector Advisory Group and market research.

multilateral alliances, soft power, and a global perspective

The goal of the global power approach to international involvement is to support its partners' objectives by assisting them in the development of their educational systems and by providing some of the knowledge and resources needed to do so. This plan aims to encourage the expansion of the international education market and education exports.

The campaign aims to successfully implement the Girl Child Education Challenge program and a variety of bilateral education projects by mobilizing expertise to ensure that nations deliver high-quality education.

One method that helps to achieve this broader global reach and open opportunities for the growth of soft power and international engagement is the export of education. Especially when other countries could profit from the knowledge and best practices in

quality assurance, accreditation, curriculum, and teaching, assisting in forging connections.
Through international partnerships, the world power observes cutting-edge educational techniques and best practices in other nations, which informs how it carries out reform and improvements.
The world power is implementing a novel approach to math instruction in England that is based on best practices.
The concept of mutual learning and partnership will continue to be a driving force behind

international involvement as it searches for fresh opportunities and excellent examples of global best practices.

Global partnerships must include features of exchange and mobility. Enabling this flow of people in and out of the nation enhances connectedness and creates new export opportunities for our education industry.

Intercultural exchange fosters relationships in academia, business, politics, and diplomacy on a global scale. Supporting students who want to study abroad helps create a new generation of people who can thrive in a society that is becoming more and more international.

Outgoing young individuals can also act as ambassadors.

The government continues to look for ways to develop a picture of the global education market and regional patterns, when the data permits, to better guide government and sector priorities.

China and Hong Kong

Government money can be given to education markets that are expanding swiftly, where there are the most barriers to entry, and where there are chances for government involvement, by giving these regions top priority. In these areas, there is also a concentration of countries undergoing educational reform, a push by governments to prioritize funding for education and research, and a need for the best learning opportunities from the expanding middle class and diversifying economies.

Place a high priority on providing financial support for educational opportunities in China, Hong Kong, and the ASEAN region.

According to ASEAN, opportunities in the ten ASEAN nations differ considerably across the region. In addition, there are other challenges. Governments can assist by illuminating and providing solutions to the issues faced by these varied countries.

promoting GREAT education

Continue to foster a welcoming atmosphere for international students while creating a more appealing program. This entails extending the post-study leave time, thinking about how to streamline the visa application process, promoting employment, and making sure current and future students continue to feel welcome.

Establish a whole-of-government strategy by putting in place formalized procedures for coordination between domestic and international government departments as well as a framework for ministerial involvement with the sector. This will be controlled by a steering committee of government representatives, encompassing other departments and the devolved administrations feeding into the current education sector.

Better accuracy and coverage of its yearly released education export data, as well as the development of an approach with an improved methodology and a wider range of sources, would help to provide a clearer picture of export activity.

Along with these prominent initiatives, the world power has also carried out several targeted initiatives to aid each area of the education sector in expanding its exporting and global presence. These steps are listed.

The International Education Strategy: Global Growth and Prosperity was published by the government in 2013. To benefit from opportunities around the world, this plan outlined a goal for collaboration between the public and

private sectors of education. It concentrated on students from abroad,

International students are crucial to the survival of some courses so that domestic students can continue to enroll in them. They also significantly increase the sector's revenue. Some of the strongest advocates abroad may one day be international students.

This plan aims to increase the number of overseas students enrolled in higher education.

Because research and education are devolved tasks, the respective strengths of the educational systems in the devolved nations work together to develop and enlarge the global offer.

Using an all-government strategy
The government is aware that for the ambition and initiatives outlined in this strategy to be successful, strong leadership and a shared government agenda are required. It must speak with one voice regarding its aspirations on a global scale and look for chances to use its resources, networks, and skills for common goals.

Chapter8

Politics and power.

It can be used either positively or negatively to refer to "the art or science of government." Positively, it can be used to allude to a "political solution" that is reasonable and nonviolent.Different approaches have fundamentally different views on how the idea should be applied, including whether it should be applied normatively or empirically and whether conflict or cooperation should be given more weight. Many different ways have been used to define the term.

A variety of tactics are used in politics, including swaying public opinion, haggling with rival politicians, passing laws, and using both internal and external force, including wars with rivals.

In modern nation states, Members of a party typically hold the same views and are in favor of the same legislative changes and political figures. Elections are typically battles between competing parties.

A framework outlining socially acceptable political procedures is referred to as a political system. Political thought can be dated to early antiquity thanks to key works like Plato's Republic, Aristotle's Politics, Confucius' political writings, and Chanakya's.
LStates became involved in the regulation of labor force markets early on and frequently sided with capital to encourage rapid accumulation. When state

abstention and voluntarism theories were popular...

The civil services were becoming autonomous organizations that were not bound by the traditional rules of government. The sociologists Max Weber, who criticized the bureaucracy of imperial Germany, and Robert Michels, who established the "iron law of oligarchy," are both associated with this point of view. Michels' Law states that every...

There isn't nobody in charge. There is no longer a centralized power, such as the federal government, which is a common feature of international politics. Each country has the authority to choose its own domestic and foreign policies thanks to its sovereign rights.

In contrast to sovereignty, each country is on its own, even with any help it may get from allies and international organizations. The term "anarchy," though it is formally used to describe this, does not necessarily imply "chaos." The system is very organized since most nation-states uphold international law. However, there is no recognized authority enforcing the laws.

Every country works toward what it sees as being in its best interests. For example, North Korea believes possessing nuclear weapons will increase their authority in the international system and act as a deterrent against a

On the other hand, nation-states occasionally flout international law and violate the sovereignty of other countries. For instance, China has illegally captured seven islands, built military bases, and claimed 90% of the South China Sea since 2015 while disregarding the rights of seven other countries. In spite of resistance from a number of its allies and without the U.N.'s approval, the U.S. invaded Iraq in 2003. Russia invaded Georgia, took over the Crimea, and took control of a chunk of Ukraine. Israel has built hundreds of unauthorized settlements in the West Bank. No international law enforcement exists to stop any of these.

Nation states still control the world stage.

Perceptions have an impact on reality. Perceptions have the power to shape reality. In order to organize and occasionally distort reality as they observe the world, leaders at all levels of government utilize filters.

Because perceptions are also based on prior experiences, we occasionally interpret other people's actions negatively while hoping they will perceive them favorably. China experienced 100 years of encroachments, military humiliations, and exploitation at the hands of arrogant Westerners and Japanese before becoming powerful and independent in the late 1900s. They still carry mistrust for the West and want to regain the power and prestige they had in the 1600s. As a result of massive casualties from decades of conflict, Russia is scared of invasion.

Conflict and Teamwork. We take covert cooperation in the international system for granted. On the other hand, disputes affecting business, security, and other concerns receive a lot of attention in the media. There are still a lot of armed confrontations despite the fact that the majority of these are resolved through diplomacy.

Transition and consistency. Despite the fact that things are changing more quickly and frequently these days, many things stay the same.

Today, travel is so accessible and commonplace that regular people fly abroad for weekend getaways, trade makes up nearly half of the global economy, and global Internet connectivity is so pervasive that a recent TV commercial featured several men from various countries competing in a video game.

how your personal experience with world politics is affected. Domestic and private issues have an impact on how politics are currently playing out around the world.

The typology of power and the results of polarity are highlighted in this section. The chapter's goal is to put current events into perspective in terms of power and polarity. This demands that concepts like hegemony, unilateralism, and multilateralism be taken into consideration. The many types of government, including both successful and unsuccessful democracies, are also taken into consideration. In order to comprehend power and trends, the Middle East will be used as a case study of a regional system of power interactions.

Chapter 9

kinds of "Hard" and "Soft" power

The distinction between hard power and soft power is crucial to the discussion of international relations. Hard power is the use of force (or the threat of using force) in conjunction with the application of financial or military resources. Additionally, it is based on resources that can be seen, like the size of a state's military or nuclear arsenal. However, soft power is the ability to influence or appeal to others. Unlike hard force, it is based on abstract concepts like culture and philosophy.

Professor Joseph Nye is the one most associated with "soft power." Nye defined soft power as the ability to shape the preferences of other countries without using force. In contrast, using hard power involves imposing one's will on others through the use (or threat of) force. Nye (1990) made the concept of soft power well-known by examining how policy was changing. Since then, the concept has been further developed as an essential element of global politics, power dynamics, and foreign relations.

Decision-makers now employ the concept outside of the academic community. The idea has gained more credence because of a soft power index that ranks each state's capacity for soft power.

Hard power is a more conventional definition of power

politics. Hard power refers to the use of economic and military might to sway other international actors. As the term suggests, hard power is the use of force to influence other agents' behavior. The ability to utilize "carrots and sticks" to get individuals to comply with demands is known as hard power. The former consists of financial incentives, but the other is a grave and serious existential threat.

The binary debate that dominates our understanding of international affairs is reflected in certain ways in how hard and soft power are conceptualized. The assumptions that support discussions of brute force form the basis of the realism perspective. Realists contend that a country's capacity to influence others to take actions that advance their particular interests results from its actual resources. States' only means of ensuring their survival is through the use of armed deterrence. They must also form coercive partnerships with other individuals. In anarchic systems, states must abide by the maxim "if it seeks peace...

From a slightly different set of presumptions, soft power is born. Due to its emphasis on actions that might create a better world, it is somewhat liberal in perspective. Instead of a hard-headed realist perspective of international relations, the emphasis on volunteer programs is more in line with a liberal worldview. Having said that, the term "soft power" is more descriptive than normative. Both democratic and autocratic governments can effectively use soft power.

A lot of variables affect both hard and soft power's effectiveness. The legitimacy of the threat itself is crucial in both situations. Given its massive military capabilities, it is completely conceivable that the US

The legitimacy supporting the exercise of power should be taken into account as another dependent component. In order for an organization's efforts to be successful, they must be seen as legitimate.

The availability of resources is another aspect to take into account when assessing the efficacy of hard and soft power. Only the richest states have the resources to keep up sizable armed forces and/or exert economic pressure on others. But smaller nations are forced to rely on their soft power. There are currently more than 36 nations without an army to protect their borders.

Time should also be taken into account in this situation. Hard power can be mobilized more easily since material resources can be moved along rather fast. This typically indicates that short-term hard power is preferable. Soft power's persuasive component is much more difficult to create because of how elusive it is. Hard power involves compulsion, yet the behavior of individuals who are subject to it is unconscious. Soft power, on the other hand, subtly and wholly voluntary affects attitudes. Contrary to coercion and conflict, consent provides a considerably more stable long-term foundation for the successful use of power.

It is generally acknowledged that the effectiveness of soft power has been aided by the shifting dynamics of international relations.

The strategy that uses soft power is more successful since it lasts for a long period. The capacity to persuade people to join your cause is a considerably more obvious example of how politics works in the age of globalization.

The US-led invasion of Iraq served as a vivid illustration of the shifting nature of power. The

Finally, the phrase "smart power" is being thrown around more and more. The ability to mix aspects of hard and soft power in ways that reinforce one another is known as smart power. The US effort to increase its footprint in Africa is an illustration of smart power being used effectively.

Great powers are those that are acknowledged to have the potential and ability to exert their influence on a global level. Three factors—power capabilities, geographic considerations, and status dimensions—are traditionally used to describe the status of a great power. A great power should hold and exercise influence inside the interstate system in terms of its spatial dimension. This aids in differentiating a regional power,

Even though the term is inherently debatable, these three factors typically make it clear who the great powers are. For instance, great powers like the economically developed governments regularly convene in a formal setting. Great powers also have a substantial amount of military, economic, and diplomatic influence.

However, there is disagreement among nations regarding the precise definition of a great power. "The great powers are an exclusive club of the most powerful states economically, militarily, politically, and strategically," asserts Milena Sterio (2013, xii). Five characteristics of a great power are outlined by Kenneth Waltz (1993) from a neorealist perspective: population/territorial size, resource endowment, economic potential, political stability, and military prowess. In an 1833 essay, the German historian Leopold von Ranke (2011, 43) stated that a great power "must be able to maintain itself against all others" during the nineteenth century.

Due to the lack of a precise measurement, despite the fact that each input is helpful, none of them fully describes the situation. As a result, there are a number of ambiguities given here. In terms of their economic strength, Japan and Germany, for instance, may both be regarded as great powers (Gunning and Baron 2014).

Despite this, neither nation has a seat on the UN Security Council that is permanently filled. Considering their respective histories, neither nation presents a strong military presence abroad. Additionally, India should be classified as a great power, according to Mohan Malik (2011), despite the fact that it is frequently categorized as an emerging power.

The nations and groups that can be categorized as great powers change over time. China has advanced significantly in recent years in terms of both its economic standing and military prowess. Due to this, some have made the prediction that China will one day be considered a superpower and that the balance of power in international relations will tend toward bipolarity.

Superpower is first without equals, not just first among equals. A superpower struts about the international stage as the hegemonic state. Although there is frequently a clear and overt emphasis on the former, their power comes from both hard and soft power. It is the only nation that satisfies the requirements.

Only one state is, by definition, a superpower in a system that exhibits unipolarity. There are two superpowers present in a bipolar system. There were two opposing superpowers with distinct spheres of influence throughout the Cold War. An ideological conflict over humanity's very future affected global politics.

Russian political and military power also offers some counterbalance to American hegemony. The United States' capacity to push its particular agenda in the Middle East is constrained by the Russian Federation's military presence in the region.

To understand modern international relations, the concept of a "potential superpower" is helpful. In terms of the economy,
It's critical to understand that a superpower's ability to influence others through coercion or persuasion is severely constrained.

Considering a typology of states, it's crucial to keep in mind that overlaps frequently occur. Based on its economic strength, China is regarded as an emerging superpower. It is confusingly categorized as a great power or superpower at times. In a similar vein, the Russian Federation was established as the Soviet Union's successor state. Although Russia is frequently referred to as a great power, it is also considered an emerging power.

The Effects of Power Structures on Polarity

The many ways that power is allocated among the states in the international system are referred to as polarities. Although states are typically referred to by the term, international organizations may also use it. There are three basic types of polarity, and knowing the differences among them has an impact on the stability and peace of the world. Unipolar, bipolar, and multipolar polarity dynamics are these three polarity dynamics modalities.

It is crucial to define stability within the framework of international relations in order to provide an accurate assessment. In line with neorealism Donald Waltz

Chapter 10

Integrity and sincerity In leadership position

The world is brimming with ambitious political leaders, but

sadly very few matchups to the traits of good leadership. In fact, many political leaders appear to be severely lacking in some of the most essential qualities of a good leader, such as integrity and accountability. It's no coincidence that the word "politician" has many negative connotations. But experience tells us that there is only a handful that comes near to the principles of leadership and shows strong indicators of a successful political leader.

Political leaders are vital – they determine the allocation of power and money through governmental policies, establish partnerships with other stakeholders, and make decisions that can have a major effect on a nation's well-being and its citizens.

Political leadership requires a leader to focus on a country's long-term betterment, above and beyond any short-term personal gains. Strong political leadership requires a mixture of charm and honesty, and the capacity to evaluate a circumstance and make a judgment based on what will be better for the majority.

Above all, leadership in a democratic system needs statesmanship – as compared to just becoming a 'politician' – which implies possessing the honesty and ability to stand up for what is fair, even though it means resigning a government post or losing an election.

What makes a good political leader?

A person with good political leadership skills will prove to be a successful leader who can easily distinguish between success and failure. A successful leader has a visionary dream and understands how to turn his visions into success stories in the modern world. Let's look at some of the skills required to be successful in political leadership.

Good communicator

communicate the vision clearly to the team and tell them the strategy to accomplish the goal, effectively communicating the message to the team, and be a good leader. Words can get people motivated and make them do the unimaginable.

Integrity and sincerity

A strong leader must have integrity and honesty, in that order. If you disregard these traits, how can you expect integrity from your supporters? Leaders succeed because they adhere to their core values, and that is impossible without ethics.

Decision-maker

A leader should be able to select the appropriate course of action when necessary. The decisions made by leaders have a significant impact on individuals. Before making a decision, a leader should give it careful consideration, but once made, they should stick with it.

The capacity to motivate others Convincing people to follow a leader is arguably the most difficult task. Only by setting an unambiguous example and motivating followers will this be accomplished. When times are rough, we look up to them and see what they can do. Think positively as a leader, and let your behavior reflect your optimistic outlook. A leader should maintain composure under pressure and maintain some level of motivation. If you excel in motivating your coworkers, you will easily overcome every challenge today and in the future.

execute delegation tasks well

Effective leadership requires concentrating on core responsibilities while delegating the rest. By this, I mean giving your followers responsibility and authority. When you try to micromanage the populace, distrust may rise and, more importantly, you won't be as motivated to work on important issues as you should be. It is important to assign the subordinates various tasks and monitor their performance. Give them all the resources and assistance they require to achieve the goal, and let them take on responsibility.

leader with a clear mission and vision. They are able to envision the future and share their aspirations with their supporters. Their supporters could comprehend where they are going if they could grasp the bigger picture. A strong leader explains the rationale behind the direction they are taking and outlines the strategy and course of action to achieve the goal.

First and first, a political leader should represent their

government, not simply themselves. Given that politics may be difficult and dirty, a strong leader must strike a balance between doing what is right for the country and upholding the adage "the nation before self." Therefore, if necessary, a political figure will be able to act harshly in the interest of the nation. A leader should be able to spot confident, unique sector specialists. More importantly, a leader must understand when it is wisest to respect authority. Leaders will possess the necessary knowledge to make timely decisions based on solid judgment.

A democratic leader should also be aware of the advantages and, more crucially, the disadvantages of democracy. He should also lead, respect, and listen to his followers while fostering teamwork and mutual accountability. A political figure should also take part in significant events both domestically and abroad. This is crucial because the leader will build significant networks and knowledge with other world-class leaders. In a word, a political leader needs to have a global viewpoint.

The nation should be united by a common thread of good administration. Have you thought about how that remark relates to the citizens' and your organization's culture? Today's prosperous nation is powered by a dedication to effective governance. Modern governance is enabled and encouraged in a country with strong governance leaders.Having a modern perspective on governance enables nations to quickly adjust to shifting conditions so that they can endure and prosper.

Recognizing effective government officials makes people feel proud of their careers, strengthens their ties to the country, and fosters a relationship of trust with their superiors.

Governance Leaders Exist at Every Level of the World Your country should have leadership at every level.

Chapter 11

Strong Leaders Are Required for Modern Governance

Good governance is supported by strong leaders. Every country has rising leaders, and they thrive on being recognized for their efforts.

where shareholders' rights, board diversity and independence, and compensation were used as metrics for measuring governance practices,

It is neither sensible nor beneficial to leave developing leadership qualities to chance. Great countries need great leaders who comprehend contemporary government, have the appropriate resources at their disposal when making decisions, and take full advantage of every opportunity. The collection of digital solutions that make up Governance Cloud by Diligent Corporation has the appropriate tools.

The leader invites a select group of workers to their headquarters at the end of each week to recognize and award those who have worked the hardest and best displayed their leadership abilities. Employees receive tangible awards, monetary rewards, or promotions as thanks for their dedication. Top executives can use their expertise to enhance working conditions as necessary.

It is evident that all citizens must act as leaders. It also shows that when leaders are dedicated to good governance, they can appoint people to nearly any job across the country and at virtually any level.

Leadership in governance is the readiness and capacity to assume responsibility for a region of the country and to consistently act in the country's best interests. A strong set of governance principles serves as the cornerstone for effective business leadership. They make decisions in accordance with a clear mission and future vision. Citizens who adopt these ideas will inevitably grow into leaders. Leaders frequently possess a few key qualities. They communicate in two directions really well. They are also very good at establishing teams and have high emotional intelligence. They have a thorough understanding of the market and are open to ideas and remedies. Additionally, effective leaders have empathy for others and know how to communicate it. It requires guts for leaders at every level to stick to their principles of justice, openness, and doing the right thing in the face of shifting or difficult conditions. A leadership quality that leaders may cultivate in their people is courage.

Team-building abilities, empowerment, trust, and a readiness to listen to proposals with an open mind are essential qualities in governance leadership. Being readily available and open to receive criticism is a crucial component in helping citizens develop these qualities.

Why It's Important to Honor Governance Leaders

The premise that honoring governance leaders improves other countries is supported by research. This book claims that praise for a job well done at nation building from one of their superiors

It's challenging for many people in leadership roles to have faith in their constituents. They might not realize it, but respect for employees is the first step in building trust. Simply expressing gratitude for the hard work they put in each day will go a long way toward creating a trusting atmosphere. People sense a deeper, more powerful connection to the country when they realize that their efforts are benefiting a cause and that senior officials have taken notice of it.

Chapter12

the avoidance of conflict

Conflict happens when individuals' perspectives, values, understandings, and mental processes diverge. Conflicts begin when people's beliefs and concepts are fiercely opposed by one another.

Conflict has been seen to occur when government organizations have contrasting perspectives and are completely unwilling to compromise.

Anytime a government body is unwilling to accept the middle path approach, conflict can begin anywhere.

Conflict leads to verbal spats, physical assaults, tensions, and relationships that are ruined.

The question "How will this fight benefit the nation?" should be considered before commencing any conflict. "Will it offer the country any solutions?"

Conflicts don't produce anything positive or useful. Simply said, it is a waste of time and resources, so every government entity should make every effort to avoid confrontation.

keep your emotions under control. Never overreact or become very agitated because this causes nations to flounder.

Never forget that other countries may not be as educated as you or come from the same background as you, but it doesn't give you the right to mock their ideas.

Be a patient and effective listener. Take close note of what the other country has to say before adding solely your knowledgeable observations. Even if you disagree with the other nation's proposals, talk it out rather than starting a conflict. To achieve a settlement, both nations must attempt to make some compromises.

Conflicts must be avoided at all costs because they simply increase a nation's concern. Never be dogmatic about anything; instead, be open-minded and seek out an alternative.

Develop the ability to control your tongue. One must reflect before speaking. Avoid shouting on people needlessly because it not only detracts from the atmosphere but also spreads a lot of negativity. When speaking to others, lower your voice and practice adjusting to their needs. Sit down with the other country and work to resolve your differences.

Be very specific and transparent in your talks because miscommunications can also lead to conflicts. Be precise in your communication and never use words carelessly to prevent misunderstandings.

To avoid misunderstandings that could lead to a fight, check with the speaker to make sure they have understood everything as intended.

Effective communication can significantly lessen the likelihood of conflicts. Never presume that a foreign country will understand everything on its own. It is your moral responsibility to make them aware of your expectations for them.

You have no right to criticize a nation for exercising its right to free speech. If you respect other nations, you will be respected in return. Always address the entire group at once if a disagreement emerges between group members. The challenges and problems must be discussed in public

.

Building resilience and preventing crises or conflicts

The rights articulated therein both identify the root causes of various conflicts and provide workable solutions by actually bringing about ground-level change.

Conflict and insecurity are frequently rooted in human rights violations, which eventually result in additional human rights violations. Due to this, approaches to peace and security based on respect for human rights also profit from this potential. As a result, defending and expanding human rights has a built-in capacity for preventing conflict. There is substantial evidence demonstrating that countries that defend and protect all human rights are less likely to see conflict.

Human rights, averting war or crises, and promoting resilience
Our strongest tool for prevention may be the Universal Declaration of Human Rights and the treaties that were created as a result. The rights articulated therein both identify the root causes of various conflicts and provide workable solutions by actually bringing about ground-level change.

In order to solve pressing issues inside or between nations that, if not addressed, may lead to conflict, the normative framework for human rights provides a strong foundation. It has not yet been fully appreciated how useful human rights information and analysis may be as a tool for early warning and early focused action. Understanding how initiatives to advance rights-based development might aid in achieving the Sustainable Development Goals is crucial since safeguarding and promoting human rights has a preventative effect.

Favoritism and bias must be absent from a peaceful environment. Only after hearing everyone's opinions should a decision be made. Lead by example and encourage everyone to follow. Remain calm and collected.

If you've messed up, just say so without feeling horrible about it. Never be hesitant to acknowledge your flaws. Be the first to apologize. A small amount of remorse can go a long way in easing unnecessary tension and addressing issues.

If the other country is too demanding, pushy, or simply unwilling to listen, it is best to avoid them. You can't win everyone over; instead, develop skills for interacting with nations that are rigid and always ready to battle.

Don't be concerned with what others are saying about you all the time. Never act in a way that you don't think is proper; don't only rely on rumors.

No one wins a battle, and you lose everything. According to the adage "Prevention is better than cure," a conflict must be prevented before it deprives a person of their mental peace and harmony.

Rapid response operations seek to increase stability and security while aiding the affected nations on their path to peace by addressing the root causes of conflict and instability. This can be done in a number of ways, such as by preventing conflicts through mediation, negotiating and enforcing peace agreements, reintegrating people, Flexibility is necessary since each crisis situation necessitates a different response that is based on the specifics. As a result, quick response actions may take many various Awforms, depending on what is necessary in each specific situation.

Respect for human rights is the cornerstone of both sustainable development and preserving peace.

Human rights have the best chance of preventing conflict when they are upheld, respected, and protected. Economic, social, and cultural rights can be just as important as civil and political rights in that they can act as both triggers and causes of crises and conflict.

Another crucial element in conflict or crisis avoidance is the pursuit of eradicating all types of prejudice and lowering inequality. According to Pathways for Peace, "some of today's greatest risks of violence stem" The idea of non-discrimination in human rights aims to guarantee that all people have equal access to those rights and that progress in realizing those rights reaches to all, especially the most disadvantaged or vulnerable. aims to abolish discrimination in all of its manifestations, with a focus on concerns like gender equality, racial discrimination, disability rights, and the rights of indigenous peoples. This promotes social cohesiveness and lessens actual and perceived injustice by addressing these issues.

Human rights prioritize persons. Better results are obtained in combating the immediate threat when responses are guided by and respect human rights, such as by ensuring universal access to healthcare and safeguarding human dignity. But they also draw attention to the most affected individuals, their circumstances, and available solutions.

Human rights serve as a guide for how States should utilize their authority so that it is used for the good of the people and not for their detriment. Human rights can assist States in recalibrating their response strategies during a pandemic to enhance their ability to combat the disease and reduce its negative effects. The three objectives are to increase the efficacy of the response to the immediate global threat, lessen the crisis's overall effects on people's lives, and prevent the emergence of new issues or the escalation of current ones. All three factors contribute to placing nations in a better position to rebuild for everyone.

Chapter 13

Top three most powerful nations in the world.

The people's republic of CHINA 0.07

Russia 0.07

United state of AMERICA 0.07